ACCEPTING
LIBERATION

What Really Matters for
Baltimore & Beyond

LIZ MATORY

DEDICATION

I dedicate this manual to our former selves. Thank you for allowing us to see more and choose better for our lives. Without you, we would have never had the courage to persevere and prosper. We are grateful for your willingness to let go and let us seek comfort in our liberty.

CONTENTS

ACKNOWLEDGMENTS

Firstly, I thank GOD for everything.

And my parents. My mom has been such an amazing blessing. Life after Pops has been life altering for us, but I am so grateful for every moment and adventure we have shared.

For my heart, my cup runneth over.

I thank all of my campaign supporters and those who have supported my media projects and writings. You have encouraged me to accept that my voice needs to be heard. Cheerleaders throughout.

Thank you for my brothers and sisters in Christ. For your fellowship, love, and prayers.

There are a few people I have never met before, but they have been the much-needed catalysts to help me level up this year: Praying Medic, Wes Brown, Ed Mylett, John Assaraf, Dr. Joe Dispenza, Mel Robbins, Jen Sincero and Rachel Hollis. Thank you for taking time to figure stuff out and for sharing your findings with the rest of us.

I also would like to thank The Heritage Foundation and the American Enterprises Institute. I am so honored to be a part of the next generation of patriots to help us remember who we truly are.

Lastly, I want to thank Arthur C. Brooks for challenging me to Love my Enemies. Having gotten so close to the precipice, your words got to my conscious just in time.

AUTHOR'S NOTE

Throughout this writing, I will be 'addressing' the Black community and issues facing Black people. Clearly any of this can be applied to anyone, and that's just it. But, it is rather a challenge for me since I do believe that race is a social construct and hyper focused attention placed on "it" has become more detrimental than beneficial in recent years. Having said that, after spending two decades of change advocacy, it is clear to me that we need to address the elephant in the room. Most of the readers may not identify as "Black" and some of the concepts outlined may be novel to you, but you too need to know more to understand better. It is also clear that context is key if we are to achieve our desired future.

And what is the future we all desire?

That is the query.

ACCEPTING LIBERATION

Liberation [ˌlibəˈrāSH(ə)n]

= the act of setting someone free from imprisonment, slavery, or oppression; release.
(*Oxford Dictionary*)

ACCEPTING LIBERATION

PREFACE

By the time you are reading this, our nation may be in the midst of a civil war or a prolonged political coup or perhaps everything has gotten back to normal as if nothing went awry.

All the more reason, this message needs to get out there. As with my previous books, there is a point in time when I can no longer ignore the idea. I have to let her out of my mind, put pen to paper, fingers to keyboard, and focus to get the message out.

This book is perhaps even more dangerous than the previous ones, so all the more reason, *Excuse* and *Anxiety* have done their best to try to keep the book hidden within me safely, away from both cynical and welcoming eyes. But we are in a state of emergency. There is no doubt about that. At no time before have we been in as much danger of losing our lives and our posterity than now.

For the last two decades, I have been on a quest to find sustainable solutions to the issues that have gone unaddressed for generations: poverty, racism, inequality, Learning, etc. These concerns are most certainly shared by countless others, but there are still very few individuals who have experienced the entire political spectrum and have come to the same conclusion that I have. After 20 years of advocacy, and almost a decade now actively fighting within partisan politics, I believe that the subsequent theories that I will present to you are the key. If other writers have stated these concepts prior to, I appreciate their efforts, but from where I stand, until we achieve full liberation, we will always fall victim to external forces and fall short of our greatest potentials. As individuals, as community, as a nation, and yes, a world.

But first thank you.

Thank you for taking the time to read and for having the ability to consider new possibilities.

Not everyone is willing to invest the time and energy to read these days. The death of the newspaper is perhaps the greatest tragedy of modern democracy, and we've accepted this reality without protest or action. They say if you want to hide a message, put it in a book. Oddly, when I have a really big message to convey, I have to write a book. That way, the message gets shared as far and wide as it can be taken. Once the book is written and published, the message has a life of its very own.

Books are still a class of their own, even in the era of social media. Nothing beats a book, and yes of course, I am biased, but in all seriousness, if you consider the logistics, the moment that a book is published every word, every sentence, paragraph, chapter, and every concept will be available for someone else to read and ponder. A book is not dependent on an algorithm. It is not held back by the editorial board. It is simply dependent on the author and the reader to take the time to connect and comprehend on their terms.

That is who we are, and this is what we are doing. I am so grateful that you have taken the time to think with me.

We will cover some ground in this little book of ours, but its mere existence is a prime example of the power of the mind. If anything, I wish to celebrate us. Right here. Right now. I want to cast a little glimmer of light in this perceived time of darkness. My greatest prayer for this little book is that it will spark what I have seen in every community meeting or conversation on the street, and especially, brighten the light of the eyes of children who have their lives ahead of them, but carry the weight of the world on their little shoulders.

But I admit my guilt.

I am being selfish as I write this book. I'm only writing this because I think it's important. Every time I see a headline, news story, hashtag, post or discussion, I see how many people do not understand fundamental principles of being. Very few people seems to understand it, and folks seem to not have space to listen. People act like they have no time to think.

Let us be optimistic then. Let's be open and conscientious just for the heck of it. Lean into our full rebellion against this cynical world we've found ourselves in, and together accept our full...

LIBERATION.

PART ONE
This Moment Now

ACCEPTING LIBERATION

1

BALTIMORE & BEYOND

A lot has been said about the state of Baltimore and every major city in America.

Entire careers and elections have been launched into the stratosphere after exploiting urban decay. Situations placed on social media have ignited communities and movements to demand radical action. There is so much exposure, but no real, tangible, sustainable resolution.

I will state something from the start. I'm not from Baltimore. I'm a DC native, born and raised. I never thought I would be nominated to congress from Baltimore, let alone live there. But I would not be able to get to this point of my understanding if I did not leave one for the other. Baltimore has always been on my radar as an especially important place. I knew that by growing up in DC, I lived within a bubble. Regardless of how influential that bubble is on the rest of the world, so much of it is not real. Some people are aware, acknowledge, and attain more information. Others may never admit that they need more. I knew there was more to the picture, and every step I took outside the DC Bubble, I could feel my knowledge and admiration grow. As brief as my time was there, Baltimore will always have a special space in my heart, mind, and spirit. And I know there is much more to it and other cities than people give it credit for.

Forever, Baltimore seemed farther away than it actually was from DC. It was just on the way to New York. It was where the Orioles played or where the big toll and tunnel were when you travel up I-95. It felt like a world away even though it isn't physically that far. I, personally, had not spent much time there until I served as a field organizer for the Maryland Democratic Party in 2014. When I was assigned to manage one of the Baltimore County field offices, I jumped at the opportunity. At that time, I had no relationship to Randallstown. Towson and York Road meant that I went the wrong direction on 695. I didn't know that the county and city were so different. I had no idea that there was a "West," "East," or even Northern Baltimore. Like most people, the

Inner Harbor was all I ever knew before then.

My other connection to Baltimore was through Mayor Kurt Schmoke. He was the dean of Howard University School of Law, my alma mater. I have the great fortune of having him as my main political mentor. Perhaps, he felt like I was like his little sister since my oldest brother and he attended Yale together. Yes, my odd relationship to generations will play a major role in this manual. I am both a millennial and a baby boomer. But many times, I heard over and over again, Mayor Schmoke was the last good mayor of Baltimore. And I so wanted to try to see if I could help address some of the persistent problems of the city. It was a dream of mine to figure out some way I could try, and when the opportunity ever arose I would be so amped.

When I got a chance to work in the Baltimore area after business school, I could sense that the rhythm was different in Baltimore. Folks are good solid people, and most people are only one generation away from their parents barely making it. Most everyone has a bittersweet relationship to the city. Since most of what was there, left with the steel mill and the economies that surrounded it. There is no pretense about anyone. No one thinks they are better or worse than anyone else. Everyone can relate. But, there was a certain edge to everyone, regardless if they lived in the "good" part of town or the "not so good". It did not take me long to understand what that energy was. Baltimore and its surrounding outskirts are metallic, tactile, and real. The city has a beating heart and everyone through their family is connected to its core. There is a lot you get to know about people when you are a field organizer for major campaigns. Since you are the one who is spending most of your day connecting with the voters (most candidates just show up after everything's set up), it's the campaign workers who really get to understand what folks are dealing with in their day to day. Every single person regardless of "skin color" or economic status wants to live their lives and be able to provide for themselves and their families. But there was always something missing in each of the interactions I had. Everyone had a different "answer" to how we could "solve" the problems of the city. And by now, most people can admit that politicians have had a long time to figure things out.

With an evaporated industry and corrupted government, on this side of things, I wholeheartedly believe that The Government cannot solve any of the real problems. I have been that person too thinking that I could help by being in government. We have seen some messed up situations and think we can try to "fix things" by becoming elected. The current reality can leave the most optimistic person disenchanted and could lead people to give up on the city. But Baltimore is more than a city, it is a shared state of mind. By that theory, then there is hope.

There is no reason why there should be as much poverty, illiteracy, and economic instability in any corner of this country (and perhaps the planet). Information has grown in an exponential rate, yet why are there so many missing pieces?

The thing with Baltimore as with a lot of urban centers, most of the population has moved out of the city by now. According to the US Census, Baltimore had 593,490 people in July 2019. In 1950, the population was 949,708. There is no middle class in the city. Just the really rich and really poor. Newsflash: race does not translate to rich and poor. Half the population regardless of "race" moved out into the suburbs. The people who couldn't leave didn't and the people who could afford the gentrified regions live wherever they wanted. Everyone invested into something. Some people sought to create the best life for their families. Some had the means to invest in entire neighborhoods. But people also invested in toxic behaviors that restricted their ability to live and prosper. These dynamics exist everywhere, and the more expansive the area, the greater impact decisions have downstream. When our country decides to invest elsewhere resources leave and so does capital. Without capital, the city continues to spin out of control.

This is the question: where is our focus? Whatever you place your attention on, that is what you will see. Baltimore can heal itself, but only if Baltimore demands better for itself.

That is not a statement just for one city, but for every city. As Ronald Reagan said, "we cannot let our desire for Government to help us blind us to the great power it has to harm us." (*Republican presidential nomination speech*, 1980). We have been blinded by that power, and we must teach ourselves how to help ourselves.

We deserve prosperity, fulfillment, goodness, and joy. No government can ever provide these endowments. We must govern ourselves to create them for ourselves.

--

We have always been connected to something greater, but it's in our nature to think small.

2

THE UNFORTUNATE DOWNSIDE TO "RACE CONSCIOUSNESS"

Before I go any further, I should give you a little context about my relationship to Race Consciousness and the Civil Rights Legacy more broadly. If it were up to me, I would use the term **Race Appreciation** not consciousness. My family is one of those families that "the media" tends to gloss over and politicians treat as unicorns. But families like mine are everywhere, and we are in our 2nd/3rd generation of economic mobilization. My paternal grandfather left Mississippi during the Great Migration for East St Louis, Illinois. He became a shoe cobbler and was able to send all of his children to college (Tuskegee and Howard Universities). My father, William Earle Matory, Sr, M.D., was born in 1928 and my mom, Rita Rigor-Matory, M.D., was born in the Philippines (not going to say the year), but she

11

became a naturalized citizen here in 1981. Her father was a military officer in both the Philippine and American armies and survived the Bataan Death March. Mom's mom was a pharmacist and was able to nurse him back to health. Both my parents have advanced degrees and dedicated their careers to the medical fields through clinical work, surgery, and education at Howard University Hospital and Howard University College of Medicine. Both led GOD-centered lives raising children over the 50s/60s/70s (my dad) and (70s/80s/90s/00s) Mom and Dad. These children went on to be a plastic surgeon, a cancer surgeon, an anthropologist, a Marine, and yours truly. There are now nine grandchildren and by next year (GOD willing) five of them will have graduated from the top universities in the world. If you were to believe the headlines, my family isn't supposed to exist, but we have for a while. And countless others. And that's important.

Growing up we were very much aware of our heritage and identity, but there was always a greater focus than just our 'race'. We were brought up to invest in ourselves, so that we could contribute fully to society. Perhaps it's because by birth I am not just one or the other, but a super intense mix. I have always been aware of how "race" impacts not just conversation, but identity as well. To this day, when I say "I am Black", I automatically "erase" my mother's heritage. I can't say I'm Asian either because that ALWAYS comes with "the look." What I have found helpful through my journey is to appreciate heritage and living life aware of our branch on the family tree. Every single one of us is responsible for how we conduct our lives, and our lives are what speak volumes. We were always mindful of not just our heritage, but our legacy. Our present was our gift from the past. It was (is) our responsibility to pay it forward into the future.

I do wonder if the people who came up with "race consciousness" ever thought that it could be detrimental to the very people they thought it was to uplift. I'm not talking about heritage, upward mobility, positive accolades and accomplishment, or innovation. All valued and invaluable to appreciate a better sense of self. I am talking about the emphasis placed on "race" in particular. Based solely on external factors and constructions, "race" has nothing to do with the power of the mind and spirit. Race consciousness, particularly in its most recent iteration, actually has become rather

disempowering.

So dangerous and damaging to the individual and community psyche that I'm not going to elaborate on police brutality, white supremacy, white privilege, systemic racism, or oppression. Every last one of these ideas are tactical tools, weapons really, of the mass destruction of our modern society.

What I would like to point out is that we are the only people who take the pain of our past and bring it through us to infect our future. Of course, we all should appreciate our history, but all of a sudden, why are people acting like we just got emancipated yesterday, like there was no progress forged over the last century and a half, like Barack Obama was the only glimmer of hope that Black people had in this country, and that we are living in the most racist time in our history? So much has happened through emancipation and now, so why are people thinking (and acting) so poorly?

Just in the last few years, I have heard time and time again that because the Constitution was written by white racist slave owners that did not include "us" when they wrote the governing document that it does not apply to "us" now. As if we are never to remember that there was a deep debate as to the language of the text, and even then, some founders did want to include more "people" within the document. They knew that these issues would later have to be resolved (and they were), but we all must remember that they were fighting for their own lives to garner freedom from the largest tyranny on the planet – The British Crown. Not to mention, they lost their fortune and lives in the process to create an entire new civil society. The civil society that we <u>are</u> a part of. We are to disregard the fighting of the Civil War and the changes to the society that stemmed from said war. Then there was that 100 years of steady, yet hard-fought progress established by two generations of our fore mothers and fathers. Forty years hence forth equality was actually realized just in time to have beneficiaries bemoan liberty or ignore its existence even though they are drenched in it. **How can people so free presume that they are not?**

We can blame the education system, the government, media, or anything else. All I know is, however it happened, we need to free ourselves of such limiting beliefs. Immediately! Like yesterday. Because if we do not, we run the risk of losing more than our lives. We may even lose our future.

For some reason, the current iteration of the Civil Rights Movement is not the same as the beliefs of the Civil Rights Movement. Now, the current view is that prior movements were insufficient or did not go far enough for what is demanded now. And what is that demand? Are mandatory classes to children teaching them that they have privilege based on their whiteness going to get us to a desired result? It seems a bit ridiculous to prescribe a false belief on someone else who does not have that belief in the first place. Is oppression of someone else the way to relieve your own feeling of oppression? Do you have to damage someone else to remove your own pain?

Thinking is being.

Who in the world told you that you (that we) are inferior?!?

Who made you think you were not good enough?

What makes you think all 'White People' got it better and that your skin color is who you can't get ahead?

Our very way of thinking and viewing ourselves is more powerful than any policy or preconception placed upon us. We are in a perpetual cycle of identifying ourselves with a fallacy and we must stop that now.

We have come to believe that our problems will be solved by a statement that was promised to us by someone on a campaign trail. Nine times out of ten, they just say things to get and stay elected.

Are we stuck? Are we really subordinate? Are we so incapable of determining our lives that we must depend on The Government or we will perish? The answer is a resounding NO. No campaign promise or government policy will empower you. You must empower yourself. We are better and more powerful than what we give ourselves credit for.

Are we aware of the signals that we are sending out to the world? Do we realize that we are proliferating fear, anxiety, animosity, anger, insecurity, and a lack of self-worth? This is exceedingly difficult to admit. To admit that this is how we feel about ourselves AND about other people with different skin color are ways that we actually have continued to think. We are doing more of day in and day out with no seeming end in sight. We don't realize that by identifying with these beliefs about ourselves and others we are relinquishing our power to someone else. And in many ways, there is no one identifiable person, but merely an idea. Disempowering as it is. These are ideas that are so powerful, they have the ability to destroy a century of growth and eliminate liberty as fast as you can hit {send}.

Do we desire better for ourselves and others? Are we sincere about wanting better lives? Or do we want others to suffer as we have so that we can feel better about ourselves and our insecurities. Now is the time to be honest. Do you believe the rhetoric, or do you believe in yourself?

Why can't people get beyond this point? More concerning is how did people who did not originally think this way, all of a sudden adopt this worldview when they did not grow up thinking like that at all. For their entire lives they lived freely and with every opportunity to soar even higher. Living with every blessing afforded to them.

We need a new direction. A new way of thinking about ourselves and the world. In many ways, it is an old way of thinking, but has been forgotten within one generation.

At first, I thought I was just leaving one political party for another. Partisan politics is not enough. But while I was on this path, I did not realize how much different my new worldview was from the previous. It even took me a while to shed the old way of thinking and sometimes I notice it creeping up, but now that I know more, I understand that there was a process that I had to actively participate in. I could not "blame" other people for not immediately understanding what I was saying or offering. I had to come to terms with the fact that there had to be another way (extra-political) to help people see more of the truth. To help with ACCEPTING LIBERATION.

The only thing worse than being blind is having sight and no vision.

– Helen Keller

3

THE NECESSARY NEW CONSCIOUSNESS

You don't have to think or look that hard to see that there needs to be a different way of thinking and being. Especially, if we want more for our life, our family, community, country, and world. I have ended up in tears of frustration and anger after participating in community events trying to encourage people to be free. Why do people continue to go down paths that they know do not serve them well? I had to check myself because I too had to figure out a better way of being because I could no longer live with the pain, anxiety, and frustration.

It may appear like we have kept personal development and community development separate. But, technically the two have been interconnected this entire time. It's just recently where we have thought that the two are separate. Even when you look back at the iconic debates about Black Empowerment, W.E.B. Dubois & Booker T. Washington, Martin and Malcolm, the discussion was over the means of fortifying the human dignity of the Americans who were descendants of slaves. **How ought The Liberated fully live.** In 1964, Malcolm X was talking about a "self-help" program and a "do-it-yourself philosophy." In his *Ballot or Bullet* speech, he stated:

> *Once you change your philosophy, you can change your thought pattern. Once you change your thought pattern, you can change your attitude. Once you change your attitude, it changes your behavior pattern and then you go on into some action. – Malcolm X, The Ballot or the Bullet* speech, March 22, 1964

The idea of competent contribution was at the core of the matter. As Booker T. Washington stated, "No race that has anything to contribute to the markets of the world is long in any degree ostracized." (Atlanta, GA 1895). Translation: When you have something useful to contribute, society needs you. We are liberated to express our creativity in the most impactful manner. People make up community, and how we perceive ourselves is at the core of who we are. Anyone who has spent any time in politics or community organizing eventually gets to a point of utter frustration feeling as if things aren't getting better, or in many ways, appear to be getting way worse despite best efforts. Particularly with so much access to information and exposure. Issues that could be 'swept under the rug' cannot stay covered for long. At the same time, with technology we expect everything to change quickly, immediate gratification. At a neutral level, prior tools and techniques may not have as much of an impact in our world. On a more loaded level, perhaps the traditional go-to tools were never supposed to solve anything in the first place. They could have been used for bandages and stopgaps to appear to do something, but really just pushed the cans down the road.

So now we have cans piled up so high that they are now a mountain. But the strange thing about this mountain is that it could have been moved a long time ago. When we are being honest with ourselves, if there are any persistent problems, the solutions lie within us, not on the outside.

Traditionally, the church has been the conduit for addressing our internal world, but unfortunately, in 2020, corruption has rocked our faith and our faith houses. By the Grace of GOD, our faith has grown since the pandemic, but the growing trend over a couple of decades is the rise of the 'nones' Americans who lack religious affiliation, believe nothing in particular or do not believe in GOD. The largest portion of our population are younger millennials, the Americans born in the 1990s. These individuals are now in their 20s. This all according to Pew Research Center. A 2018 Newsweek article points out that there is a rise in witchcraft, pagan, and pre-christian religions. For your information, that is tarot, astrology, covens, hexes, and spirit conjuring/worship. And I should point out all that places attention and seeks to manipulate the external world, not appreciation of the internal and eternal. When you overlap the narrative of a "white Jesus" or that "Christianity doesn't celebrate women" you find even more "Black people" rejecting the Bible or being more susceptible to false idolatry.

Sadly, even the Pope has conjured up a way to neutralize traditional understanding of family and responsibility to proliferate "solidarity" as the new buzzword. In his letter to the 2020

General Assembly of the Organization of American States, he spoke of expanding the love that we have for our nuclear family to the broader community. We are to be responsible for the comfort and livelihood of everyone, not just our families in the name of "solidarity." That is socialism straight from the Vatican. After Brazil, Mexico and the Philippines, the United States has the most Catholics in the world at 77.4 Million. That's how many people who believe that the pope is the representation of God on earth, and that's how many people may receive a socialist message straight from The Holy See. It's eerie to see how stealth communism has become that the church and in turn churchgoers have so easily accepted a doctrine that rejects the very existence of GOD. It blows my mind to see how many people are willing to accept a philosophy that hunts out anyone who practices Christianity for the sole purpose to kill and intimidate anyone who believes in a power other than government.

So, no wonder we are off kilter. We have drifted off course and our churches have been at the helm. If we cannot rely on our churches to lead us properly, then we must rely on ourselves to harness our faith from within.

Make Room for Better.

We have to let go of what is not serving us.

Letting go can be difficult, especially when folks tell you to "get over it". Like that is super easy for someone else to say. They didn't go through what you went through. They don't understand, right. It's easy for someone else to look from the outside in and tell you to let it go. Because underneath that statement is "it's no big deal, so why are you making it such a big deal. What's your problem?"

But what if that's not what letting go or getting over something means? What if you think of it as focus and energy? You may be focusing on something too much. Or perhaps, you can shift your focus a little (or a lot) and see things a little differently. That new way may give you a little more room for a more helpful energy around the situation. This new way will get us more room to breathe.

When we focus just on the bad things, or on something that didn't go the way we wanted, we limit our view to that particular understanding. But often times (all the time) there are life-changing experiences just around the corner that we may miss if we don't push forward and walk passed and let all of us change directions. When we stay in that one reference point, we automatically get stuck and there is no possibility for better. Regardless of what you deal with, you must leave space for better.

4

WHAT IS THE "ASK"?

You have heard *ask and you shall receive,* right?

Well, just in case you need a reminder, it goes like this:

> *Ask, and it shall be given you; seek, and ye shall find; knock, and it shall be opened unto you:*
> *For every one that asketh receiveth; and he that seeketh findeth; and to him that knocketh is shall be opened.*
> *Or what man is there of you, whom if his son ask bread, will he give him a stone?*
> *Or if he ask a fish, will he give him a serpent?*
> *If ye then, being evil, know how to give good gifts unto your children, how much more shall your Father which is in heaven give good things to them that ask him?*   *Matthew 7:7-11 KJV*

When you really pay attention to this passage in the Bible, the LORD is saying that he will give you all that is good that you wish. And since he is the Great I AM, the request will not be what a normal father would give, but something greater than anything we could ever imagine.

As individuals we can take time to think about what we want. We can pray and focus our attention to anything and everything that we believe we want/need. We believe that GOD will grant us the good gifts that we seek when we go to HIM. But what about our community? Why wouldn't we expect the same for more people than just us? Do we not have enough faith to believe that HE can do good things for the rest of us too? (Hint: GOD not Government)

But have we ever asked what we wanted from GOD? Seriously. Particularly for our community? If we are serious about creating better for us all, what do we really want?

Ask:

1) What would it be like to ...?

    a. have every child read well and could focus well enough to learn in school?

    b. walk down the street and feel safe in my surroundings?

    c. have gainful, wholesome employment for my neighbors and friends?

2) What is a better way to be?

3) What if my community was like this, living in this reality?

4) Who in history do we admire, and what were the traits they had that we admire?

(Questions adapted from Breaking the Habit of Being Yourself by Dr. Joe Dispenza)

These questions remind me of how community used to be. First, we did not have to look far to see examples of lives we admired and wanted to emulate. Everyone lived among and around each other so even if you did not have good role models at home, there were other people around. Personal integrity, responsibility and honor were the core to living a good life. These values were never considered offensive or undesirable. That was how you were raised and that's how you expected to live your life. More importantly, you wanted to live your life in a manner that you could be proud of. Even if you didn't have a lot growing up, you were going to make a better life for yourself AND give back. We were responsible for ourselves and each other. Government never came into the picture.

I know I sound like an old timer, like *back when I was growing up*...but oddly, it was back when I was growing up, we did have a better understanding of our personal responsibility, and in turn, we were more optimistic about our future and our lives. I had mentioned previously, my father was born in 1928 so I learned this from him. When he imparted his sage advice on me, I used to think that he was so old school and I thought that it was different for my generation. Of course, I had to grow up to understand what he really meant by all of what he said, and when he transitioned, life gave me some clear examples of *oh that's what Dad warned me about. Totally, should have listened.*

The good thing about development is that you are always developing. And isn't that Life. Dad would say, "It's the follow through that counts." The first part of that statement is actually, "when you're shoveling $___, it's the follow through that counts." Translation: when you are dealing with bad stuff, what is important is what you do afterwards. And even though at this time I've only literally shoveled a couple of actual piles of manure. He was right! Follow through does matter. You have to really get underneath and push through making sure you don't step into any more manure. Sometimes you have to go through another pass to get more of it up, but lucky for you, there's less of it this time. And most importantly, you have to have a place to get rid of the stuff. You have to discard the crap. Bonus, manure can be a good fertilizer providing necessary nutrients to let flowers grow.

5

GETTING UP AND OVER IT

My First Time

I will never forget it.

The first time I began to notice my thinking around race was an actual thing.

It was a family gathering in Pennsylvania. I believe it was an anniversary for my aunt and uncle. The gathering was as normal as it could have been, but it was different than any time before. The sisters were busy in the kitchen helping out with the event. Even though there was a caterer, my mom and her sisters were always hosting and helping each other out. So, I naturally just did what I watched them do over the years and I lent a hand. I grabbed a tray of hors d'oeuvres to hand out to the guests on the back patio. Outside of my own childhood home, this house was one that I spent the most time visiting since we all would make a point to stop

there on the way back and forth from DC to
New York during my college years. We would
pass Baltimore and head up to Philadelphia. I
was comfortable and felt very close to those
particular aunt and uncle. But the moment I
walked out, tray in hand, and presented the
food to the guests, I freaked out.

All I could see was a sea of white folks,
and none of them I had met before. I
immediately had this thought – *Oh, gosh! They
think I'm the help.* I immediately went back to
the kitchen where my aunts were and started
crying. One of my aunts, Tita Marie, (God rest
her beautiful soul), quickly said to me, *"What
are you upset about? You are a lawyer and our
niece. Besides why do you care what others
think of you?"* I knew what she said was right,
but I could not get beyond how that moment
made me feel. It was the first time I noticed
being the "only one" at a family function since
my father had passed away before that
gathering. For my life prior to, I made "more
sense" when both of my parents were present.
People, once they met us, they understood the
relationship because they could see us with
their own eyes. Like *"Oh, we get it, your dad's
black and your mom's from the Philippines."*
But after knowing that my dad wasn't there and

he would never again be physically present with us, I felt random all of a sudden.

Of course, we are not the only ones who can be "considered the help". Don't forget Americans of Filipino heritage as many other immigrants can be seen as such by some people as well. What was different is that they as immigrants did not allow someone else thought to impact their own sense of self. We have developed two distinct ways of thinking and I was the one who suffered because of my feelings. That immediate, visceral reaction I had, I will never forget. And for a while I could not get over that "fear" of experiencing it again. The next time I will watch my reactions/responses was to decide specifically that my race and other people's perception of my race, could not control me. Sure, there are plenty of times when your 'spidey senses' are going off for a good reason, but it does not serve any of us to live our entire lives on high alert for a potential threat that may not exist. Especially, when particularly now that we are well into our liberation. It is our duty now to not relinquish our identity to someone else's preconceived notions about us. **We are in control.**

Control!

Yes. I was a Janet Jackson fan (and a Paula Abdul fan) growing up. So, shout out to Miss Janet. Control!

No in all seriousness. Who is in control? Are you? Are we? Or have we relinquished our power to someone or something else? I think now is as good a time as any to ask who or what is controlling us?

Stop, and really think about it.

I'm the baby of the family, so I didn't have that much say on what I got to watch when we were growing up. My brother was in control of the remote. No cable so there were only but so many options in the first place, but I watched a lot of He-Man, GI Joe, Star Trek, Dukes of Hazzard, and the A-Team. I may have been able to sneak in a Smurfs once or twice and if I was lucky, Jem! But seriously, if we're talking about our programming, who controls us?

First, we need to be aware of the fact that we are in control. GOD has created all of us to have control of everything in our body from the moment we are born. Sure, there are some times and some situations where we are dependent on something else, but if we are healthy, we control our bodies and at the very essence, we are in control of our lives. But when we start from that initial understanding, we have a great perspective. When we are aware that we are in control, we then can figure out how to change things that we may not want and exchange them for something better.

Doomed or Destined.

We are not only predicting the future based on the past, we are presuming that it is inevitable and out of our control. As far as I know, we are the only people in history who have used the pain of our past to dictate our fate while having the means of breaking free. Honestly, we are free already.

Helplessness. Reaction. Control. Powerlessness. Habits.

Lower vibration. Denser. Heavier feelings. Many of us move through this world as if we have the weight of the world on us. That weight is debilitating, and it paralyzes us, restraining our ability to think clearly and live freely.

We are constantly living in stress. Financial insecurity, health issues, biological toxins ingested in our food, water, and air. Some of us are surrounded by physical and mental violence. Even just through our rhetoric we can believe that the entire world is out to get us. This is no way to live.

You might have heard of "fight or flight"; it is when your brain perceives that a danger will cause harm to your survival. Your body goes on High Alert. Your heart begins to rise, and adrenaline increases to prepare to defend you from the danger or run away. When our system is under stress constantly, we are not able to rest and eventually this stress impacts our health. We develop **dis**-ease (disease). In addition to disease, we actually become addicted to the sensation of stress. And we end up seeking out situations that give us that high that we crave. Drama.

Interestingly enough, according to Dr. Joe Dispenza, we are the only living things that can create stress simply through our thoughts. We do that by worrying about the future and revisiting the past over and over again. We begin and then constantly think that what happened in the past will happen in the future, and we take all the feelings/emotions from that memory and recreate them in our present state.

"Living in survival causes us to focus on the .00001 percent instead of the 99.99999 precent of reality." - Dr. Joe Dispenza

We literally think ourselves out of health and into disease like cancer, colds, arthritis, heart disease.

- According to the CDC, the number one cause of death in black males under 45 in this country is homicide.
- Heart disease is the number one cause for black men over 45. For Black women, the leading cause of death is cancer from 45 to 84.
- Heart disease is the leading cause after that.
- The suicide rate in young people under 24 increased by 60% from 2007 to 2018 according to the CDC.
- The National Coalition Against Domestic Violence says that 1 of 4 women and 1 of 9 men experience domestic or intimate partner abuse.

- 322 million people around the globe suffer from depression according to the World Health Organization.

Bottom line – everyone needs to change their state of being because our lives depend on it.

Part II

METHODS OF THE MIND

ACCEPTING LIBERATION

6

POWERFUL STUFF

The following breakdown will come from two particular texts and philosophers: 1) <u>Breaking the Habits of Being Yourself: How to Lose Your Mind and Create a New One</u> by Dr. Joe Dispenza [Dr. Joe] and 2) <u>Innercise: the New Science to Unlock Your Brain's Hidden Power</u> by John Assaraf [John]. Both men have done a lot of research over decades and have created centers/programs to help individuals develop more fully. I will attempt to relay their theories here in this context. These theories make a lot of sense to me particularly after 20 years of political advocacy. While I was navigating my own self-development, pieces started coming together and I do believe…

The starting point is our brain.

Oddly, even the perception of our brains has a "racial" history too. Eerie as it sounds now, but pseudo-scientists for hundreds of years used scientific racism to create/validate white supremacy. So, when I tell you the origins maybe you'll understand why I am so against the notion of white supremacy and racial inferiority in the first place. One of the most notable "studies" was conducted by Samuel Morton in the 1800s when he studied the cubic inches of skulls of 'Caucasians', American Indians, and Black Americans. His findings stated that 'Caucasians' had the larger skulls and Black smaller. This was then used to assume intelligence and skull size were related. Larger was thought to mean smarter, which then translated to capability and comparison based on "race".

Too bad for these real-life racists our brains are the same. All we need to learn across the board is how to master our minds. If we do not take an opportunity now to begin to understand our power and accept liberation, we have the potential to see liberty slip away.

Thoughts. Words. Feelings. Actions.

Pops would always say, **"A man thinketh so is he."** Whenever I was having one of my moments, he would say, *"A man think so is he."* It is amazing to learn that my father was right this entire time, but it took me to actually read the Bible to know where he got that from [For as he thinketh in his heart, so is he (Proverbs 23:7)]. In recent times, we have heard the words "consciousness" and "awareness" all the time now, but the true meaning of the notions have not really seeped farther into societal conscience as they ought to. If our brain is one of the most complex creations ever, then of course, it will take some time for even humans to learn more about how we actually function.

Both John and Dr. Joe talk about the chemical and hormonal activity that occurs within our brains when the experience certain things. Every time we have a thought, a chemical reaction occurs in our brain. Signals are sent through our brains when we respond to certain experiences. Our brains are responsible for keeping us alive, and so when information enters our brains, we evaluate whether there is a threat to our lives or not. Anything that is not familiar to us, can be considered a risk. Familiar experiences, surrounds and thoughts make us feel good. And so, we repeat them to stay in our "comfort zone."

John discusses conscious and subconscious. The subconscious brain runs on autopilot. There is no need for thinking, like your heart beats and you know how to walk etc. But the conscious mind is a higher, more sophisticated part of the brain that actually is aware and thinks.

Below is a chart that John uses in his <u>Innercise</u> book:

Your Conscious Brain	Your Unconscious Brain
Super Slow	Lightning Fast
Conceptual	Perceptual
Thoughts and feelings	Instinct and emotions
Deliberate	Habitual
Explicit	Implicit

Breaking down some of these words, our conscious brain is the thinking part and the unconscious brain is reactionary.

The left = purposeful

The right = automatic

We can, over time, retrain our minds to form better habits, but that change will be perceived as different, a threat, and in turn be rejected by our unconscious. The reactions of that part of our brain are mood swings, anxiety, fear, stress, excuses, overwhelm, lack of focus and organization, confusion, lack of energy, excessive procrastination, and lack of personal peace (Innercise, p. 28). When your brain feels balanced, you are organized, clear headed, happy, confident, performing at your best, and are emotionally grounded. (Id.)

When you take a moment now, think about how you are feeling. Are you feeling balanced and organized, confident and happy OR are you anxious, full of fear and stress? Are you making excuses or suffering mood swings?

Ok. Stop right there.

This moment you just took is a major step. When we are able to focus and evaluate where we are and what we are thinking we activate our consciousness. Consciousness is just awareness. Without it, you are not paying attention. With it, the attention allows you to stop, think and evaluate. That is the power that no other being (that we know of) has. That is our superpower. Dr. Joe talks a lot about the power of attention in his book, <u>Breaking the Habit of Being Yourself: How to Lose Your Mind and Create a New One</u>. If and when we want to change our lives to a better way of being, we have to change how we are. And in order to change how we are, we need to be aware (or conscious) of how we are, what we think, and how we feel first.

"How we think and how we feel create our state of being." – Dr. Joe Dispenza

Thoughts are the language of the mind

&

Feelings are the language of the body.

It is this relationship that we negotiate to create different outcomes. All of it is energy, and you can tell, especially if you're feeling a certain way. When you're angry or anxious, you can feel it. When you're happy and content, you can feel that too. Unfortunately, we may have experienced more "bad" feelings than good these days, so you may be able to recognize them first. But the good thing is, you are noticing them. That is powerful.

What you need to then do, when you want to feel better, think or do better, is to be intentional with what you want. Want peace of mind? Then calm your mind. Want love? Then feel love. Want more? Then feel/think/be grateful.

Memorized Emotions

EMOTIONS	FEELINGS	EXPERIENCE
Anger	Aggression	Pain
Fear	Frustration	Suffering
Envy	Anxiety	Sadness
Hatred	Insecurity	Hopelessness/Depression

Referenced by Dr. Joe Dispenza

"Warning: when feelings become the means of thinking, or if we cannot think greater than how we feel, we can never change. To change is to think greater than how we feel."

– Dr. Joe Dispenza

Dr. Joe speaks about "Hebb's Law", a brain science principle that says that nerve cells that "fire together, wire together." When activities happen over and over again, they bond together and then work in unison whenever a sequence starts. So, when we think the same way, we feel and react the same way. Then we see the world in a way to reinforce what we already know and presume. Things become subject to our interpretation not as they actually are objectively. We are just reacting without thinking. And thinking is what matters. It always has been what really matters.

We are Creators Not Mere Creatures.

The reality behind the statement that **we are creators not just mere creatures** is that we are made in God's Image. God is creation. Therefore, we are creation. No other creature (that we know of) has the power within our minds to create anything beyond the rudimentary and occasional tool. We take this ability to create for granted. We can change with our thought alone. When we think differently, we feel differently, and when we feel differently, we behave differently.

The only mind-blowing concept that Dr. Joe talks about is really next level, so you may not be ready for it. I, myself, am adjusting to it too, but I personally am ready for some dynamic change in my life. And if you are as well, consider this:

Time does not exist.

I'm not going to attempt to break down the meaning of quantum physics, but when you apply the theory to your personal system, it actually makes sense. Again, when we discuss thoughts and feelings. And we know that just a mere thought of a past experience can immediately bring back the feelings you have around it, Dr. Joe points out that your body does not know that the experience isn't happening. It thinks it is real time, even though the thought is a memory. So, your past immediately becomes your present. Your future also can become your present because when you worry about something happening that has not occurred, you are projecting a past experience into the future, and yes, you guessed it, you feel it in the present.

Our minds do not interpret what happened and what is happening. So, our memories and fears can literally affect us in the now.

What gets us into trouble is that we focus

on the body, we are always worried about an environment that we are constantly trying to escape. And it is a matter of attention and intention for us to save our lives. But what happens if the danger you fear is an ideology and not an actual physical danger. The fear only comes from the concept that you allow to scare you into submission.

These last five (5) years this caustic ideology has grown exponentially. We are inundated by negative images and situations that purposefully push us to hyper focus on our environment. 2015 – Freddie Gray. 2016 – Trump elected. 2017 – Resistance Movement 2018 – Divisive politics. 2019 – White Supremacy/Privilege assertions 2020 – COVID and Chaos. All the while systemic racism.

Honestly, it makes perfect sense why anxiety and depression are at an all-time high, but the biggest problem is that most of the fear stems from a fallacy. Systemic racism does not exist. For it to be true, everything would have to be racist. And guess what? Race is a made-up thing as well, so we are all basing our entire worldview and life on something that is not real at all. Remember, nerve cells that fire together, wire together. Our brains are stuck in this rut.

Our mind is stuck believing these lies. It is a belief system that relinquishes all power to the external world. Our entire worth is then given over to a shapeless idea. Placing such power on race and more specifically inferiority in 2020 is more destructive than times before because we are allowing the most debilitating thought to control our state of being. We have placed shackles on our minds and enslaved our possibility.

We need to be conscious of our conscious.

The system stays in place only as long as you keep it in place.

Serious question: Do you want to be happy? Do you want your family to be happy? How about your community? State? Country? World?

Are we willing to change the circuit? Have we become addicted to the reality we are in. These feelings of guilt, anxiety and being afraid of mere perception have become so familiar to us, we have grown accustomed. It is easier for us to stay where we are. Even as negative it is. Different freaks us out. What is known is comfortable. What is unknown makes us uncomfortable. As John points out our unconscious minds will fight our conscious mind and make it difficult to escape and separate from the familiar. But, when we expend energy on things that do not serve us, it takes away energy that we need for the good stuff.

It takes a conscious decision to want to think, feel, and be different. Most of our way of interacting with the world is focused on the outside. This entire discussion around race is external. We are allowing external matters to impact our circumstances, and we then have given up control of our "destiny".

"Most of us live in the past and resist living in a new future." – Dr. Joe Dispenza

The Two States of the Mind & Body

SURVIVAL	CREATION
Stress	Homeostasis
Contraction	Expansion
Catabolism	Anabolism
Dis-ease	Health
Imbalance	Order
Breakdown	Repair
Degradation	Regeneration
Fear/Anger/Sadness	Love/Joy/Trust
Selfish	Selfless
Environment/Body/Time	No Thing/No Body/No Time
Energy Loss	Energy Created
Emergency	Growth/Repair
Narrow Focused	Open Focused
Separate	Connected
Reality Determined by Senses	Reality Beyond Senses
Cause & Effect	Causing an Effect
Limited Possibilities	All Possibilities
Incoherence	Coherence
Known	Unknown

Chart from Dr. Joe Dispenza, Breaking the Habit of Being Yourself

Question: What are you relating to on this chart?

Question 2: Are you beginning to understand?

7

#BREATHE

Has anyone ever had to remind you to breathe?

It sounds odd, but I've been that person before. I'm sure I was that person for years, but in 2015 I reunited with my childhood friend and my first love, Christopher Barry. I've mentioned him throughout my writings and I'm still processing what our shared moment in time really meant, but for now, I want to tell you about the time when someone had to remind me to breathe.

Five years ago, Christopher decided to run for Ward 8 City Councilman in DC's 2015 Special Election. A special election was called because Chris's father, Marion, had passed away at the end of 2014 and the seat was left vacant. Chris and I had not seen each other for years. From age 2 to 8, we attended the same small private, elementary school where Washington's Black leaders sent their children to be educated properly by Ms. Carlise Davenport. The school only went up to the 3rd grade and afterwards, the young graduates matriculated to the various private, elite schools in the area. And so that's what happened with Chris and me. I went to Sidwell (the school of choice for the Clintons, Gores, Sulzbergers, Goldmans, Cohens, Grahams, Bingaman, Bacchus, and later, Bidens, Obamas, and Stephanopoulos). Christopher went to St. Albans (chosen by the Rockefellers, Marriotts, and Ambassador A, B, C and D, et al.). But the "Bitch Set Me Up" sting operation where his father was caught smoking crack with someone not his wife. That moment that effectively sealed his legacy to being the Crack Mayor. That event happened that school year when we were 9 (Chris) and 10 (me) years old. Marion was the mayor of DC, and from that moment our lives and how we interacted with Life began to diverge.

When you figure out that external influences can impact your mind, I have seen it firsthand with Christopher.

No one was more impacted by the dark underbelly of politics than Christopher Barry, and I did not fully understand politics, human nature, pride, ego, addiction, corruption, and the power system until I worked with him as his campaign manager. Immediately, we figured out that we had to determine who was friend or foe. Everyone has an agenda. And, it is not always one to benefit the community. For the most part, the people who we suspected were the ones we had to stay away from. Working with Christopher, I knew I had crossed a threshold, and I was very much out of my element. It seemed like every conversation I had, with every interaction, energies were off, and I was in panic mode without even knowing.

Carl, Chris's friend from middle school and our field director, knew what was going on, and he was the one who had to stop me at least hundred times to remind me to breathe. He had spent more time between worlds.

Breathe, Liz. Are you breathing?

Every single time, I had to stop and realize that I was very much in fight or flight. No, I was barely breathing.

Three key points I learned from this.

First, I had never been around so much darkness in my life. In many ways, it was everything that my father had tried to keep away from me. But when he transitioned in January 2009, I had to experience Life After Pops to understand more fully what was at play. There's only but so much you can hide your children from. We must live our lives to understand life. Yes, every single choice made has consequences. But it is how you navigate the experience that matters.

Secondly, you are never alone. Whatever you face, there will be people along your path to help you through. Even if it's a person there to remind you to breathe, the LORD will make sure you have guidance. Everything can be used for your growth. But you must step back, take a moment, and breathe. Ok, you may to take several steps and breaths, but you got this.

Thirdly, I want you to know BREATHING is powerful.

Deep, centering breaths do so many things on so many levels, scientifically, spiritually, literally, and metaphorically. If this is the only thing you remember from this entire book, know that *Breath = Life*.

8

IT'S OKAY TO BE JOYFUL

I have no idea who made us feel like we cannot enjoy our joy. But in some communities, we are led to believe that if we're happy and other people aren't happy, then we have to stop being happy because we're going to make other people feel bad. It's weird, strange reasoning. Well it's not reasonable at all to force yourself to be miserable so that other people don't feel bad about you feeling good, but this is definitely a prevalent form of thought. Wherever it came from, we need to let that Bad Boy go with the quickness.

There is a moment when your life just shifts to amazing. I thought it wasn't a thing until it became a thing for me, and to be honest, I am still in love with the amazement. Like stop you in your tracks and Thank GOD for what you have, how you feel, and love that surrounds you. Tears are no longer sadness but Warm Your Heart and Soul tears of joy. Like finally meeting the man of your dreams and catching yourself blinking to make sure that yes, he is real. He's not Prince Charming. He's a million times better. It's not that you had an actual list of factors, but if you were to have one, the list is completely checked off. His bumps and bruises match up with yours. There are things that neither of you have to explain to each other because you are a survivor too. And he wants you even still. Well, you love him even more because he looks at your flaws and sees them as beauty. But still you start to freak out because you're so not used to feeling comfort and actual love. You experienced more distrust than trust, and you fear going down that road again and again and again. You have a decision to make - Be in Love or Be in Fear. And you are ready to own your decision.

And it's not just people who come into your life from your thoughts. Dogs too. I never thought I would be a Dog Mom. Seriously, I never understood people's relationships with their pets, dogs particularly. Dad actually said when we were younger that if we got a dog, we wouldn't have any more vacations. My brother and I then had no desire to get a dog. I remember thinking dogs are dogs and people are people. Clearly that is the case. I so didn't get what the big deal was. But I was a lot more ambivalent about canines until we adopted one. And yes, now I totally understand. If I ever had a thought about owning a dog it was fleeting, but I knew that if ever a dog would be in my life that I would want a pit bull. And that is definitely the dog we got this summer!!! It has been very intriguing to live with a dog. More specifically, to go through emotional transitions. She can sense us, and she knows when we (I) need extra cuddles. I can actually see and say that my dog and love changed my life.

Joy is everywhere and we should embrace it. Because joy multiplies. Instead of hiding joy or rejecting it for fear of offending someone, we should welcome it so it can grow ever more.

9

THE DECISION IS YOURS

The decision is yours and it always has been. Will you accept liberation or reject it? We are powerful beyond our wildest dreams, but we are allowing ourselves and our "community" to cower underneath demoralizing belief systems that have done more damage to our minds, bodies, and spirits than any time before. This is an amazing time to be alive. Be serious about it. Find joy within it. And if you cannot, take the time to be deliberate with yourself and build a better life for yourself. They say, you cannot give anything you do not have already. If you want happiness, then be happiness. If you want forgiveness, then be forgiveness. If you want abundance, then be abundance.

It's okay though. There is a reason why for all of it. But we have the power within us to create anything we want. That is how GOD made us to glorify HIM. At every moment with every decision you make each day, ask yourself, are you glorifying GOD? Can the energy you give off represent the love like GOD or are you spreading something else? You can totally tell what type of energy you're giving off, especially if you are paying attention. And sometimes you may have to leave and find an entire new place for you to access your voice. Sure, you want to be able to be anywhere and radiate always. But that may not be the case until you gain more mastery of being you. This is the time to renew your now. Determine what you want and when you create your better being, you will be accepting liberation that is what really matters for Baltimore and Beyond.

SOME WORDS OF WISDOM

MOM & DAD

"It is not your aptitude that determines your altitude, but your attitude." – Dad

"There's always going to be someone richer than you, poorer than you, prettier than you or uglier than you. Don't focus on other people. Focus on who you need to be." – Dad

"Don't let people have free rent in your head." – Mom

"Don't worry about anything longer than 10 minutes. Let it go and move on." – Mom

"To thine own self be true." – Dad (originally from William Shakespeare)

"Uukol bubukol." (Tagalog for If it's meant for you, then it's meant for you.) – Mom

"Your time will come." - Dad

ACCEPTING LIBERATION

RESOURCES

The Bible, King James Version or earlier

Innercise: The New Science To Unlock Your
Brain's Hidden Power   by John Assaraf

Love Your Enemies: How Decent People Can
Save America from the Culture of Contempt
                    by Arthur C. Brooks

Chronicles of Negro Protest (Compilation)
                    by Bradford Chambers

Breaking the Habit of Being Yourself
                    by Dr. Joe Dispenza

Girl, Wash Your Face
                    by Rachel Hollis

#MAXOUT Your Life: Strategies for Becoming
An Elite Performer
                    by Ed Mylett

You are a Badass: How to Stop Doubting Your
Greatness and Start Living an Awesome Life
                    by Jen Sincero

ABOUT THE AUTHOR

Liz Matory is an author, political commentator, motivational speaker, and recovering politician. Liz spent most of her life as a race conscious liberal having grown up as a second-generation member of the Black Intelligentsia in Washington, DC. She never considered changing her political philosophy until she became increasingly frustrated with the politics of the Democratic Party.

Wanting to find better solutions to issues like generational poverty and economic instability, Liz left the Democratic Party and became an independent to run for the US Congress in 2015-16. By 2018, she became an outspoken conservative receiving the Republican Party nomination to congress in Maryland. Liz made history becoming the first ever American of Black heritage to be nominated by the GOP and the first American of Asian heritage to be nominated by either major political party to the US House of Representatives from the state. This was the same year Liz discovered she was in an abusive intimate relationship with a pathological narcissist.

By the Grace of GOD, Liz came to Christ November 30, 2018. Her ex committed suicide Christmas Eve a few weeks later.

Liz spent most of 2019 in an evangelical, independent fundamental Baptist church. Then on October 17, 2019, the iconic congressman, Elijah Cummings passed away. Wanting to further the progress of the shared community by promoting conservative solutions, Liz decided to run for the congressional seat vacated by Cummings death. Global pandemic and all, 2020 offered her another opportunity to appreciate real solutions for persistent issues.

Liz dedicates this book to everyone who finds themselves at a crossroads as well. If she can figure a way through, anyone and everyone can.

Breathe. And Breathe again for good measure.

Start building a better tomorrow, today.

ACCEPTING LIBERATION

NOTE TO SELF

NOTE TO SELF

"The problem with Race in Consciousness."

– Liz Matory

Made in the USA
Coppell, TX
11 August 2021